Pups and the Big Waves

By Margaret Whitfield

OXFORD UNIVERSITY PRESS

It's windy and rainy.

It's Zuma and Skye.

There's the boat.

🔊 Picture Dictionary

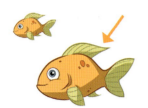
big

boat

catch

cloudy

cold

fast

rainy

wave

wet

whale

windy

Activities

1 Match and say.

2 Who says this? Circle.

I like whales!

Let's go by boat.

You're fast, Zuma!

I don't like waves.

I'm wet!

Count all the big stars in the book.

Great Clarendon Street, Oxford, OX2 6DP, United Kingdom

Oxford University Press is a department of the University of Oxford. It furthers the University's objective of excellence in research, scholarship, and education by publishing worldwide. Oxford is a registered trade mark of Oxford University Press in the UK and in certain other countries

© Oxford University Press 2021

PAW Patrol: ©Spin Master Ltd. ™PAW PATROL and all related titles, logos, characters; and SPIN MASTER logo are trademarks of Spin Master Ltd. Used under license. Nickelodeon and all related titles and logos are trademarks of Viacom International Inc.

The moral rights of the author have been asserted

First published in 2021

2025 2024 2023 2022 2021
10 9 8 7 6 5 4 3 2

No unauthorized photocopying

All rights reserved. No part of this publication may be reproduced, stored in a retrieval system, or transmitted, in any form or by any means, without the prior permission in writing of Oxford University Press, or as expressly permitted by law, by licence or under terms agreed with the appropriate reprographics rights organization. Enquiries concerning reproduction outside the scope of the above should be sent to the ELT Rights Department, Oxford University Press, at the address above

You must not circulate this work in any other form and you must impose this same condition on any acquirer

Links to third party websites are provided by Oxford in good faith and for information only. Oxford disclaims any responsibility for the materials contained in any third party website referenced in this work

ISBN: 978 0 19 467765 3

Printed in China

This book is printed on paper from certified and well-managed sources

ACKNOWLEDGEMENTS

PAW Patrol illustrations by: Nathanial Lovett

©Spin Master Ltd. ™PAW PATROL and all related titles, logos, characters; and SPIN MASTER logo are trademarks of Spin Master Ltd. Used under license. Nickelodeon and all related titles and logos are trademarks of Viacom International Inc.

Access all your resources in one place.

- Audio
- Teacher's Guide
- Parent's Guide
- Parent's videos

1 Go to www.oup.com/elt/download
2 Enter the code below. Follow the instructions.

You can only use your code once.

Your access code

Need help? Email Customer Support at eltsupport@oup.com

For customers from mainland China:

中国大陆地区的教师和家长们

Please use the following website: https://www.oup.com.cn/zh/english-learning/preschool/doraseries

请从以下网址获取相关资源 https://www.oup.com.cn/zh/english-learning/preschool/doraseries

First steps to reading success for very young learners of English

Levels

A 3-level series of over 60 graded readers – story books + phonics story books

Pups and the Big Waves

Mayor Goodway and Alex take a boat trip, but when the weather turns bad they need the PAW Patrol's help!

 Download Audio, Parent's Video and Guide, and Teacher's Guide from the inside back cover.

nickjr.tv   #709988

ISBN 978-0-19-467765-3

OXFORD
UNIVERSITY PRESS

www.oup.com/elt/gradedreaders